The Island Man Sings His Song

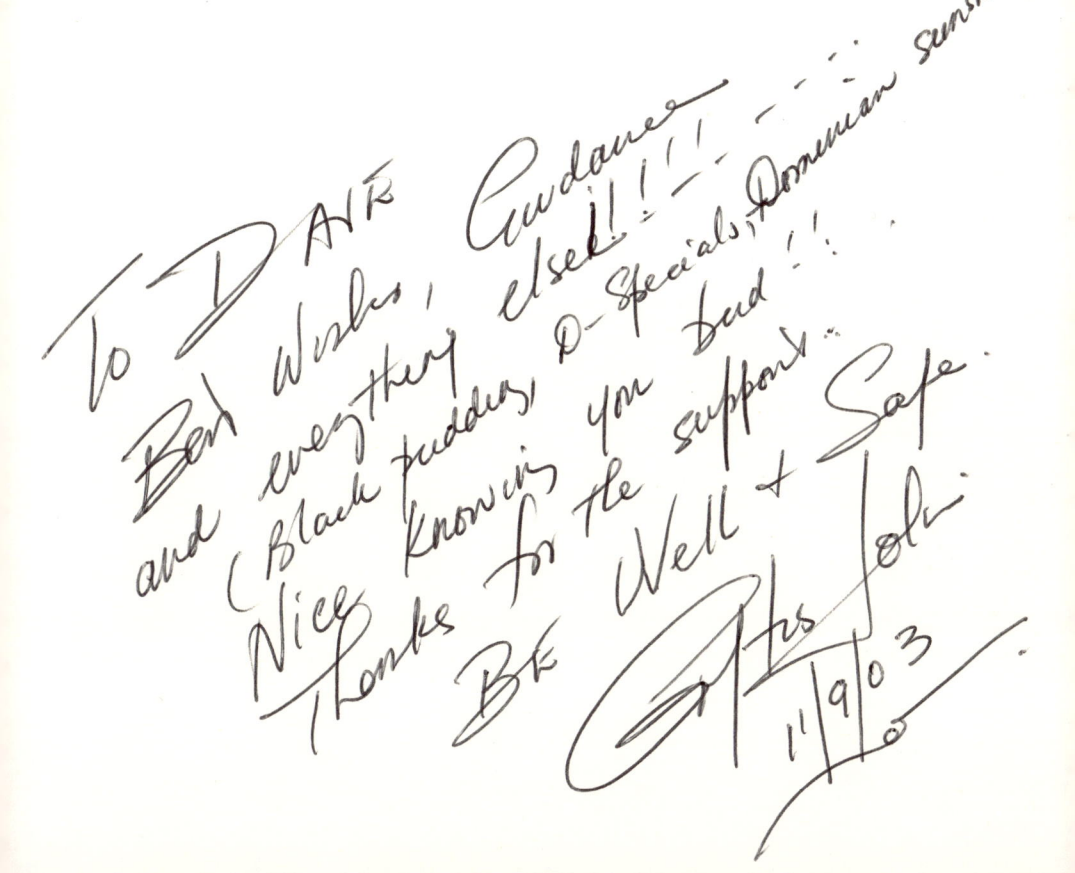

*To Dave,
Best Wishes, Guidance
and everything else!!!
(Black pudding, D-Specials, Dominican sunshine!)
Nice knowing you bud.
Thanks for the support.
Be Well + Safe.
Giftus John
11/9/03*

The Island Man Sings His Song

A Collection of Poems

Giftus R. John

Writer's Showcase
San Jose New York Lincoln Shanghai

The Island Man Sings His Song
A Collection of Poems

All Rights Reserved © 2001 by Giftus R. John

No part of this book may be reproduced or transmitted in any form or by any means, graphic, electronic, or mechanical, including photocopying, recording, taping, or by any information storage retrieval system, without the permission in writing from the publisher.

Writer's Showcase
an imprint of iUniverse.com, Inc.

For information address:
iUniverse.com, Inc.
5220 S 16th, Ste. 200
Lincoln, NE 68512
www.iuniverse.com

ISBN: 0-595-18090-6

Printed in the United States of America

I dedicate this book to my wife, Theresa, my kids Jamal and Mandisa, my parents and brothers and sisters. Thanks for helping me to dream and to live the dream.

Love You Always.
Geejay

Contents

Acknowledgements xi
The Dawn 1
Cricket 2
Deserter's Cry 4
Another Era 5
Marbles 7
The Flower 8
For A Daughter 9
Fly 10
For The Unborn Child 12
Ropes of Freedom 14
In I Meditation 15
Rain 16
Tribute to Philip 18
I Made You Cry 20
When She Cries 22
Mirrored Images 23
Are You Yourself? 25
I Saw Her 26
For I am A Dominican 28
Let Me Live 30
A Walk Among Strangers 32
Is Mas 33
Words in the Quiet Moments 35
She 36

The Island Man Sings His Song

Is this the Dominica?	38
Hurricane	41
Tourist	43
Reality	45
Sea of Disillusionment	47
Hold on	48
Wasn't it Yesterday?	50
For A Son	52
I am Afraid	53
For Our Sister	55
De Goliath	56
Let Freedom Ring	58
Snowfall	60
The Island Man Sings His Song	62
The Ghetto Song	64
Faces	66
Visions	69
They Riot in the City Tonight	70
Summertime Nostalgia	71
Who am I?	75
The Royal Palm	77
Face of Darkness	79
The City	80
The Sun Sets on A Nation's Son	83
Me Gold	85
Marooned	87
Midnight Melody	89
Am I Me?	90
A Symbol	92
The Fight Must Go on	94
New Light	96
Search	97

We're Coming Back 99
Old African Man 102
You, The Poem 104
A Confused World 105
Lord Me Wan' Pray 107
My Day 112
Play Ball! 113
The Snow Storm 115
Remembering Aurora 117
The River's Gone 119
Sunday Afternoon 121
Their Game 123
Until Tomorrow 125
About the Author 127

My special thanks to Irving André, Rocco Dormarunno and everyone who has been some source of help and inspiration which has made this book a reality.
Thanks to The Almighty for the breath of Life.

The Dawn

Slowly it climbs
See how it illuminates the sails
Out on the distant water.

Slowly it climbs
Over the still dark mountains,
Majestic and bright.

The sun rises
Shining with all its glory.
Slowly it climbs
Like a baby waking from a peaceful sleep.

Slowly the dawn conquers
Dispelling the darkness, giving hope.
Slowly it takes control of everything before it,
Everything in its path.
The dawn rises.

Cricket

The panorama of colors, dresses and parasols
Lend beauty and setting to the surroundings.
Men, women, boys and girls,
Ticket buyers and stowaways
Snuggle into wooden stands
And along the ropes on the boundary lines.

Cheers, whistles, clapping
As the crowd greet their heroes.
It's cricket! Lovely cricket!
Tension and excitement
Swaying saman trees bend and squeak;
Radios blare…
Bottles of rum
Are poured down throats
As the sun's rays sip through a mass of dark clouds.

The bowler paces, breaking into a run
His long legs covering ground easily
As he heads towards the batsman.
He jumps and delivers.
The batsman glances
And the shining red sphere flies off the middle of the willow.

A chase begins, but it's useless
As smooth leather races to the boundary lines.
More whistles and cheers, this time thunderous and deafening.

Giftus R. John

The drums beat in approval
And more spirits are drained down throats.
Parasols wave.
It's cricket man! Lovely cricket!

Deserter's Cry

I miss you
In the mornings
When the raindrops drown the roses
Their fragrance perfuming the air.
I cry alone for
I miss your love, your warmth, understanding and care.

I miss you
In the quiet evenings
When the moon glistens atop the palm fronds
Swaying briskly in the night
While the insects
Hiss their soft, haunting tunes 'neath rotting leaves.

I miss you.
I miss your warm embrace
And the feel of your fingers cuddling my body.
Your gentle, soothing touch;
Expressions of our love
And your sweet voice, whispering softly in my ear.

Like a castaway
On a lonely desert island
I remember you once again sweet one
And the thought of your warm tender lips
Pressed against mine.
I remember you today as my heart sadly grieves.

Another Era

A number,
A multitude,
A people,
A Nation,
Stand, stoop.
Clear night.
And amid the din and confusion
Another of the many flags
That have gone up and down
On this land
Goes down, finally
Marking the last stand of colonialism,
The final stanza in a blighted and torrid past.
And slowly, solemnly,
Another one goes up, for the first time.
And at that moment
The people remain
Motionless, captivated.
Then like great explosion
The voices,
The cheers,
The euphoric cries of jubilation
Rise up, filling the night
As the flag finally reaches the apex.
Commands ring out
And they are deafened.
Tears are shed
And dried.
And as this new nation is born
Questions are asked, so called answers given.

The Island Man Sings His Song

Here it is. At last. Long last!!
Independence! Yes Independence!
One day ends and another era folds up.
Another day dawns and another era
Slowly begins to unfold.

Marbles

Young boys stooping low to the ground
Playing in the rain.
Some, their bare buttocks protruding through patched pants
Skillfully twirling their fingers.
They pitch marbles
In the muddy, sticky dirt
Their shirts soaked to the skin
By the late afternoon showers.

The marbles roll on as time slips by
And somewhere in the village
Mothers shout, swear and scream at the top of their voices,
But it's all in vain.
Dirty fingers are cleaned
On dirtier pants
And the boys play their game
Pitching their marbles in the rain.

Blue, red, green, purple marbles
Each urged on to be a winner
Roll slowly on in the tacky mud as
They're pitched again and again.
Yet the boys play on
Mindless of their mothers' pleading shouts
Enjoying themselves, enjoying the moment.
Doing their thing in the afternoon rain.

The Flower

In the early morning
It stands alone
Dewdrops hang from its petals
Birds chirp their joyful notes
Bees too hum their tunes
From their fragrant pedestals
A red beautiful blossom
Like a new day
A new life
New dreams
New hopes
Its fragrance
Fills the air
Beautiful flower
Too beautiful to be moved
Too beautiful to be touched.
But alas I fear
To the ground it will fall
To be trodden upon by all
And the birds will mourn their loss
And bees will no more buzz.
And today
They will fly away
To where beauty lies
And like that flower
Man too dies
And travels to eternity
And when he does
Who will behold the beauty?

For A Daughter

May you always be happy
At the same time, remembering
Never to be dishonest and insincere.
Don't be afraid of trivialities.
Insist on what is right.
Stand firm, be strong.
Always be yourself.

Respect what is right.
Expect obstacles and criticisms;
Nonetheless be firm, be poised.
In today's world
There will always be problems.
Approach life with determination.

Fly

Fly
and when you open your beautiful wings
shelter my body
from the heat
that falls over it.
Fly.

Fly
and carry me on your open wings,
carry me
away from this depressed land
that sends me raging.
Fly
and take me with you.

Fly
and take me to your nesting place
atop those green mountains
where I will find peace
where I will be happy.
Fly
and take me away with you.

Fly
and take me on your wings
above those beautiful white clouds
to a place of sanity
a place of peace.
Fly and take me where you will.
Carry me with you.

Giftus R. John

Take me away
where I won't be lonely and depressed
for I'll find you there
to help me along.

Come, open your wings
carry me
take me away
for I want to be free.
Free from the shackles,
free from the ills of society,
free from the problems that confront me
on this Land.
Fly
Carry me away.

For The Unborn Child

Oh unborn child
Seated deep within thy mother's womb
Nourished, protected, safe and secure
What do you see?
As you roll and jump
In your dark amniotic chamber,
Waiting your day of freedom,
What do you hear?

Oh unborn child
Created out of love and passion
So tender, frail and untouched
Why do you cry?
As you kick and bang
Against your prison walls
Longing to get out of that crouch.
What do you hear?

Oh unborn child
Symbol of life's continuity on earth
So delicate, yet vibrant and alive
What do you feel?
As your mother awaits
The day of your birth
Hers to hold, cuddle, love and cherish
What do you see?

Giftus R. John

Oh unborn child
If only you could tell us
What lies hidden deep within
Your growing mind and body
Then the world would learn and listen.
Oh unborn child
Created out of love and passion
Waiting to challenge the world
Please answer me.

Ropes of Freedom

I cling tightly
To the ropes of freedom
Dangling above my head and
I try to move up to the very top.

But I am pushed down
And the ropes dangle out of my reach.
Now I am back,
Back in the place that I really dread.

Back in brutality and oppression
Back in frustration
Hatred, discrimination and racism.
But no way will I stop.

Again I try to climb those ropes
But then they are too far, too high
And I am unable to get to them
As they sway teasingly above my head.

Still, I endeavor to move on.
In a world filled with ups and downs
I will endeavor to catch those ropes.
I have not yet failed and I won't give up.

Hope still walks
Below those ropes.
The Ropes of Freedom,
Forever dangling above my head.

In I Meditation

in i meditation
i man see you free
just free
free from de struggles dat confront i an' i.
in i meditation
i man know
i an' i gonna be free, understood an' get
much respec'.
for in i an' i meditation
i an' i share dat which i need.
love.
one love.
in i an' i meditation.

Rain

Wet, mud-filled shoes,
Damp clothes,
Dripping umbrellas
At the front door,
Drenched heads
Playing,
Scampering
In the rain.
Splashing,
Giggling,
Running,
Shouting.

Over-laden clouds
Collapse
Over the dark, towering mountains;
Ceaseless noise of rain
Pattering
On window panes
And on rusty, galvanized roofs
As garbage-filled gutters
Begin to spill their contents
Unto the narrow streets.

Poorly built roads
Crumble
As swollen, rushing rivers
And creeks
Flood the land.

Giftus R. John

Creatures drown.
Vehicles roll on,
Wipers splashing,
Headlamps flashing.

People seek shelter
As herbal bush and cinnamon tree bark
Boil in black teapots
Keeping warm, the poor souls,
Trembling with cold within.
The rain continues pouring.

Tribute to Philip

Hail Philip, hail though you're dead
Hail though you're gone
Gone a martyr for the rights of this land
Your life cut short by a soldier's gun.

For your rights, our rights and freedoms
You died, gunned down;
Felled by a soldier's bullet
On that early Thursday morn.

Your blood, slowly it flowed that day
Hopefully not in vain
As next to Brother Germain you sadly died
A warrior in the falling rain.

Surely your blood did not flow in vain
A martyr for a noble cause
Like Martin and others who were shot
While "power seekers" ayed destructive laws.

Fare thee well Philip, so long brother
As dark clouds cover the land.
Fare thee well brother, fare thee well;
Justice will someday lend a hand.

The earth you shall walk no more
But your spirit will live on and on
And it shall give strength and courage
To this island's daughters and to its sons.

Giftus R. John

Rest Philip, rest brother, undisturbed
As we carry on the fight
To free this land of corruption and shame
Bringing all their evil deeds to the light.

I Made You Cry

Last night I made you cry
And today I am sorry.
Last night I made you swear
And today I am guilty.

Last night I did you wrong
I had no need to.
Last night I hurt you
And today I am unhappy.

You cried and your warm tears
Trickled down your face
Unto your hands
And remained there.

You cried last night
And your heart bled in silence
As you whispered words
Softly into my ear.

Last night you rested your face
Upon my shoulder and
I felt the warmth
As your tears wet my shirt.

Last night you cried, sweet one
Because I did you wrong.
Today I cry silently within
Because I know you're hurt.

Giftus R. John

Last night I kissed you and the salty tears
Touched my quivering lips
And I understood.
She loves me I said, deep inside.

I am sorry I whisper, hoping that you will hear.
I am sorry I scream, from deep within
Hoping that you understand, hoping that you care.
Because last night, you cried.

When She Cries

When she cries
The earth trembles
For it feels the pain
That one who resembles life itself
Undergoes.
For when she cries
The early morning flower
Weeps with her.
The cool soothing breeze ceases.

For when she cries
Life cries. Life cries
For it can't bear the pain
When she cries.

Because when she cries
The sky cries with her
And the rain falls over her
Beautiful body
And tries to hide her tears
As they trickle down her face
When she cries.

Mirrored Images

I see
Mirrored images
On the wall
Reflecting shame, guilt, oppression
Of one pushed
Against the wall
Against the glossy wall
Cracked glossy wall.
Mirrored images,
Dim mirrored images
Of innocent children
Living
Growing
Starving
Dying.

I see
Mirrored images
Of castles in the sky
Rising, rising, rising
Then crashing to the ground.
Mirrored images
Of a bright tomorrow
Darkened by war, pollution,
Greed and starvation.
Mirrored images of a lost mankind.
Hazy images
Of peace, development, and civilization.

The Island Man Sings His Song

I see
Mirrored images
Of the future,
Of the unknown
Flashing through my troubled mind.

Are You Yourself?

Are you yourself
Under the smile that you carry?
Returning a smile won't hurt
Especially if it is sincere
Illuminating a darkened mind won't hurt
Laugh and be happy. Aren't we friends?
Let your light shine brightly
Irrespective of what goes on
And I'll be happy. Be Yourself.

I Saw Her

I saw her. Truly I did
I remember I did
As she stood there
Looking like the early morning sunshine
Brightening another day
With its matchless beauty.

Truly I did. I saw her
With hair, black as the dark night
And eyes that shone like the evening stars.
Yes I did.
She was so pretty!

In all her radiance
I remember those lips
Nice wet lips.
I saw her
With a beautiful nose,
Captivating breasts and hips.

Like metal drawn to magnet
I neared closer
My heart rushing,
My eyes cemented to hers.
My legs tarried
And she was gone
As I reached for her lips.

Giftus R. John

I looked around me
But all I saw
Was the emptiness
That engulfed my room.
There was nothing in there
But total darkness.

For I am A Dominican

To you land I pay allegiance
On this day
When the pages of memory
Are unfolded unceasingly
Unto the sons and daughters
Born and bred on this fruitful soil.

Many years long past
By Columbus
You were discovered.
Now I give you allegiance
Honoring and praising you
Dear Land of my birth.

I'll sing out my heart to you
Your dear beloved name
I'll uphold on this nation's day
When we all think of you
Land so fair and young.

Yet I won't sit
And let injustice, hatred,
Greed and theft
Smear your beautiful name.
I won't sit and let
Men look down upon you.

Giftus R. John

I won't let other islanders
Shun your image.
I won't let my fellow Dominicans
Abuse your beauty,
Your charm;
For I am a Dominican.

I will go to the shows
On that day
When you are praised and honored
When your children will show
Their national culture
In songs and drama
Dear Land of Rivers.

But Land, I'll tramp you so hard
I'll forget that you are there
With a glass
And a woman
And a rum
Jump up time all day long.
Yet land
I pay you allegiance
For I Am A Dominican.

Let Me Live

No. Don't! Please don't!
My very soul cries out. From within
My womb I feel you shake, rumble
With deceit, hatred, treason.

No. Please don't!
As the cry from inside the ghetto
Vibrates within my eardrums
The cry of a people rising in unison.

No. Please don't!
As you climb winding paths,
Or trod along pot-holed lanes;
Crevices of my retarded development.

Please don't! As the claws of poverty
Tighten around my frail body
Lying midst this Caribbean archipelago,
Submerged in the Sea of Underdevelopment.

No. Don't! Please don't! As the sound of the drum
Vibrates within the heart
Of a people living in faith of the distant past
Shaking in fear of the unknown future.

No! I scream.
In the dark forests of my imagination I cry out
As the misty hills tower over a new-born child in the cold,
An innocent lamb to the slaughter.

Giftus R. John

Let me live to hear the rhythm of the African drum
Once again, to quench my burning bosom.
Let me live to be green again
And to smell the fragrance of the balizier.

Let me live
To feel the rain showers coming down in torrents
As tributaries rush down the hills and through the valleys
Of Belles, Layou, Laudat and Gleau Gommier.

Don't. No, don't destroy me!
Allow me to become stronger.
Allow me to grow. Don't neglect me.
In my fragility, hold back thy hand and believe.

Let me live to see the copper haze of the setting sun,
To hear the shrill notes of the Sifleur Montagne,
Let me live to hold you within the deep contours of my body
And to smile with hope. Let me live!

A Walk Among Strangers

Yesterday I walked among strangers
And no one uttered a word.
Yesterday I walked among strangers
Each seemingly in a world of his own.

Yesterday I walked among strangers
And no one noticed me
As each rattled on, lost somewhere,
A stranger of his own being on a crowded street.

Yesterday, I smiled at strangers
And no one smiled back
Faces taut, cold and expressionless
Filled with fear of what lies unknown.

Yesterday I walked the city streets
Bustling and alive with people
Each with a set mind; a set agenda
Each with some pressing deadline to meet.

Yesterday I walked alone with strangers
People of every nation
In a bustling, crowded, and jam-packed city
A city of such fame, fortune and renown.

Today I took a walk alone
Along a lonely, empty street
And I felt peace with myself today.
I smiled along with the silence and the empty street.

Is Mas

Jumpin', singin', movin', rollin',
On de ground.
Sweatin', shoutin', screamin',
Drunk on de road.
Their bellies got too much load
Jumpin' on de land.
Woman on one hand
Bottle of Belfast Rum in de other.
Dey can hardly stand.
Dey jumpin', dey whinin'.
Is Mas.

De sun settin'
De rum flowin'.
Monday gone,
Tuesday almos' gone.
De roadmarch refrain
Soundin' again an' again.
"Solomon roulay si nou mort
Nou mort nanne sala."
Is mas dem playin'.
Dey rubbin'.
Dey cussin'.
Dey partyin'.
De steelband soundin' loud.
Sweet calypso music in de Dominica heat
As dey move an' groove to de beat.
Whinin', chippin' down de street.

The Island Man Sings His Song

De *la peau cabrit* soundin',
De crowd shoutin',
De dust risin' in de air
An' de drum soundin' louder.
Is Mas.

"Doh hang your heart"
"Chicken bounce, chicken bounce"
"What you tryin'?"
De music stop.
De time comin' closer by de hour.
Now dey begin troddin' home.
Some alone,
Some hug up dey man or dey woman,
Some don't know which way to go.
And de music slowly gone quiet.

Dey chip slowly. Tired legs.
Mas soon done.
As dey approach de final moments,
De chants of de night
Emit from tired, hoarse and drunken voices.
"Come go home…ah nu alle
Ah nu alle ah kai mama nu"
Dey shout again and again
As de jump up come to an end
An' all pan pack up.
No more chippin' an' whinin'
An' rubbin' an' sweatin'.
Bal la fini. Tout bitain fini.
But is mas.

Words in the Quiet Moments

Words
In the quiet moments
Flutter in my mind
Like leaves in the tropical breeze.

Words
In the quiet moments
Come and linger before me
And I pluck them out carefully
And slowly, quietly
Set them to paper.

Words
In the quiet moments
Send me travelling away
From the world of torture
To a place of peace and tranquility.
Words of love
Words of romance
Words of peace
Words of unity.

For as I sit quietly
I find time to reach out
And touch
Words
And I shape them, mould them
To satisfy my inner being.
Words
Words in the quiet moments

She

She is the Queen of my life,
The upholder of my life
The breath of my life
The water of my thirst
The food of my hunger.
Yes,
She who toiled and labored
She who washed and clothed
She who caressed and kissed
She's my Queen
The Queen of My Life.

She who stands behind me
She who gives me strength
She who gives me love and wisdom
She's my Sun
The Sun that brightens my life,
The Sun that guides my life.

She who fed my hungry lips with milk
From her breasts,
She who soothed my pain
With her tender touch,
She who held me
With her safest hands.
She's my Moon
That shows me the way in the darkest hour
She who stays near while I am asleep.
She's my Queen.

Giftus R. John

She who carried me
In her protected and comfortable womb
For nine careful months
She who smiled when she saw me
She who felt proud when she saw me
She who felt proud when she bore me
She's My Queen, My Sun, My Moon, My Life.
She, whose love surpasses all others,
She's my Mother.

Is this the Dominica?

Within my subconsciousness
I see a land
Beyond the shimmering dark clouds;
An image that I once knew.
And I keep asking:
Is this the Dominica that I once knew?
The Dominica that opened her shores
And allowed herself to be swarmed
By buccaneering Europeans?

Is this the Dominica
That once accepted African slaves
And their white massas
Within her dense foliage;
Who fought and chased the Caribs
Deep within the confines
Of the threatening jungles?

Is this the Dominica
That felt her heart
Shake, ache and bleed
From the plight of the negres marron
Forever running and hiding
From the guns of their white owners?
The island that saw the seeds of revolution
Fall, and spring up again
Grow stronger, spread their branches
Then wither only to rise once again
Nourished and watered by the blood of
Mabouya, Jacko, Philip and Balla?

Giftus R. John

In my agony
In my pain,
I ask:
Is this the Dominica
Where crystal clear water
Churned on through the night
Playing soft music
To the night insects?
Where the raindrops soothe the burning flesh
When the overloaded clouds
Collapse over the towering peaks
Of Trois Pitons, Micotrin and Daiblotin?

Is this the Dominica
Where drenched heads played,
Scampered, giggled in the rain?
Where children ran along
Playing *hoop séwé*
Singing, dancing, jumping
Loving Lawan?

Is this the Dominica
Where the sound of the drum
Once meant war, vengeance
And the rich lavway went piercing
Through the dark night
Disturbing our forefathers
Resting peacefully in their graves?

Is this the Dominica
Stripped naked
By the forces of nature;
Floods, hurricanes?

The Island Man Sings His Song

Is this the Dominica
Stripped bare, unclothed,
By the hands of dishonest politicians
And their circle of opportunistic lackeys?

Is this the Dominica
That I once knew
With a God-fearing people?
A proud people?
A caring people?
A people who cared for their country
Who fought for their country?

Is this the Dominica
That I see
Disappearing slowly in the distance?
Is this the Dominica
That I once knew?

Hurricane

The wind howls,
Tree limbs snap like
Matchsticks between one's fingers.
Roofs lift off from houses
And float like kites in the air
Before crashing noisily
Atop other houses
Inflicting a lot of damage.

Blinding sheets of rain
Come whipping into rooms
As windowpanes are shattered,
Or blown out by the force of the wind.
The swollen river, now overflowing its banks
Rushes crazily along
Taking with it cattle, pigs,
Tree trunks and branches.
Nothing is spared as the swirling wind howls louder.

Galvanized sheets twist around telephone poles
Like sheets of paper around pencils.
Giant waves crash to the shore
Hoping to drag anything back
To the ocean's depths.
Fishermen's boats, their lifeblood,
Are ripped off their moorings
Splintered in seconds
As the wind growls louder
Like a hungry lion
Hunting a meal.

The Island Man Sings His Song

It's been like this for hours.
Lord when will it stop?
A chilling scream
And a house slowly crumbles to the ground
Like some huge elephant
Had stepped over it with its giant feet.
The inhabitants scatter wildly about
Seeking shelter from this monstrosity.
The darkened sky grows more frightening by the minute
As low, thick, clouds race across.
A giant breadfruit tree, now leafless
Comes crashing to the ground.

A lull, just for a short while
A tempting and eerie calm.
And then it begins all over again.
Sheets of blinding rain
Gusting, screaming wind;
Shattering peals of thunder
This time more intense and frightening
As the afternoon grows darker.
The hurricane rumbles on
As we wait hopefully for the end
And the light of day.

Tourist

Lying on the water's edge
Listening to the splash
Of the waves
On a distant alien shore.
Dreaming of oppression,
Pollution,
Nuclear power,
Or some never ending war.

Miles away from home
On a beautiful, warm day.
Like a boy
In his childish innocence
He punctuates the soft, black sand
With his toes, enjoying the freedom
As sand creatures creep along
Seeking refuge from man's ignorance.

A soldier crab
Creeps up and stops
Raising his giant claws
In defiance, protecting his turf;
Looking inquiringly as if to ask.
Why are you here?
Wanting to lay sole claim
To the black sand and the surf.

The Island Man Sings His Song

A pair of frigate birds
Circle quietly above the water
Rising and dropping
With the warm tropical breeze.
Their giant spans cast
Momentary shadows over
His semi-tanned body
As they float with such grace and ease.

The waves roll in
And the salty water hits him
As it rushes in ever so quickly
Splashing softly against his side.
A sheepish smile covers his face
As the sun glides away in the distance.
He gets up, surveys the empty beach
And rushes headlong into the rolling tide.

Reality

Alone out there
Like the early morning fog
That overpowers the jagged hills
Before disappearing into nothingness.
Deep within you surge the tides of fear and suspicion.
You, a mere mortal being. Alive
Before a raging and savage herd without the will
To fight and survive.
As you stand out there,
Out there alone, alone in your own confusion.

See, the fog hovers menacingly
And the sun loses yet another battle
Only for now though, for surely
It will only be for a while before
The fog will rise and dissolve again
As it reveals the truths. For realities
Exist not only for a while but eternally.
It's only the unreal that dies.
Look around you.
Reality is in the sun, the moon and the rain.

Fear not, my brother
For the day, the moon, the sun,
The night, the clouds, the rain
Even the fog that will hover
Like a bird of prey, are realities that exist.
Fear only thyself! Fight!
Raise your eyes. Look yonder.

The Island Man Sings His Song

Let those who have sight
Let those who believe
Behold life's reality too real to resist.

Let not your thoughts be filled with doubts
You hear me! Nor let it
By your own trivialities, be buried
Too deep within that foggy shroud
That continually veils your mind.
What do you hear? A sparrow!
And what do you see? A flower in bloom!
Or smell its fragrance as it is carried
By what little breeze blows?
Life is alive my friend. Don't be blind.

For what is man who knows reality?
What is he? Another statistic? No!
But a symbol of God's creativity
Performing his part on life's daily stage.
He comes and goes, forever.
Yet life continues its journey
As we ride nonchalantly, morning, noon and night
Happily tagging along
Enjoying the free passage.

Coward! Quit not.
Don't give up the battle
Do not relinquish your hold
Of what is good and true.
No damn it. Don't! For quitters, they die young
Not innocent, but guilty.
Have faith in yourself.
Believe in yourself and what is good.
And be happy with yourself.
Life is good my friend. Live it! Be strong!

Sea of Disillusionment

Cascading
Over sharp edged rocks,
And down through deep gorges
My thoughts flow on
Bouncing against boulders
And thick tree stumps
And fall down, noisily.

The rush is over
And I settle down
For a while
In deep blue pools.
And then my thoughts flow on
Rushing, splashing
Along rocky banks
Wildly.
My thoughts flow on
And on
Into the Sea of Disillusionment.

Hold on

Face the music
Stay in there, face the crowd
For it's rough out there.
Stay strong and stand out proud.

Don't panic
Move slowly with the beat.
Hold on! Hold on!
Don't fall off your feet.

Hold on, stand firm, be true
No longer is it what it was
No longer is there food to eat
But bombs, guns and wars.

Today seems like a saddened child
Whose dreams have vanished.
No more the breath of fresh air.
Life's no longer dearly cherished.

Everywhere is the stench of pollution
Who cares for our salvation?
Toddlers are becoming parents.
Oh what a mass of confusion!

Fraud, greed, corruption run amok
Along the pot-holed lanes of life
As the powers of darkness keep growing.
Lord, it's a world of strife.

Giftus R. John

The world writhes as the beauty disintegrates.
Is it worth living?
Be bold! Be brave! For behind the dark clouds
A bright light is glowing.

Wasn't it Yesterday?

Wasn't it yesterday
That we ran along the backyards
Playing games, laughing in the rain
Unashamed of our own nakedness?

Wasn't it yesterday
That we sat in the moonlight
Listening to grandpa telling stories
Of laugarou, soucouyan, and la diablesse?

Wasn't it yesterday
That we fought each other
And our parents flogged us
Whether we won or lost the fight?

Wasn't it yesterday
That we were boys, just boys
With patched pants and shirts
Running in the dark, narrow alleys at night?

Wasn't it yesterday
That we bathed in the sea all day
Diving and swimming, having fun;
Enjoying ourselves till the sun went down?

Wasn't it yesterday
That we climbed to the top of the hills
And raced each other with our scooters
Mindless of the heat from the blazing sun?

Giftus R. John

It was yesterday, wasn't it?
When we skipped school and played truant
As we roamed the hills above the village
Searching for guavas, nuts and berries.

Oh how does time fly by
Aging and robbing us all
Of the good times of yesterday
Robbing us all of those fond, sweet memories.

How does time fly by
Changing the things that
We once loved and lived for everyday;
When we were boys, just boys.

Today, they are just things
That we can dream of as time moves on
Like the sweet moments of yesterday
When we were boys, just boys.

For A Son

Just remember as you trod
Along life's pathways, that
Many have traveled those roads
Albeit seeking the best that
Life has to offer them.

Strive my son, for the best
Hold on dearly to what is good
Even though it may seem trivial.
Relinquish not your hold as you
Wrestle with the evils of this world.
In the end you'll be proud you did.
Never doubt life my son. Be Yourself.

I am Afraid

I am not afraid
Of the man who despises me
Because of the color of my skin
Or just because he simply hates me.

But I am afraid of you
Who calls me brother
Yet you rape, stab and kill
Your very own black sisters.

I am not afraid
Of the man who despises me
Because in his confused mind
A free man, I don't deserve to be.

But I am afraid of you
To whom I offer my hand
Yet you mug and rob me
While I at the bus stop stand.

I am not afraid
Of the creator of *"white flight"*
But of the fear and tension
I feel from my own brothers at night.

I am afraid of you
Who from me a dollar beg
Yet returns the favor by
Slamming a bullet into my leg.

The Island Man Sings His Song

I am not afraid
Of the man who calls me any name,
Boy, bastard, darkie or nigger
As he plays his racist game.

But I am afraid of you
Who asks "How you doing brother?"
Yet in that same breath
Refers to another as "that nigger."

Yes I am afraid of my own black brothers
Who fail to see any value
In what Martin, Malcolm and others did
Sacrificing their lives for me and you.

Yes, when they gave it all up willingly
So we may get to where we are today.
When with their lives and their blood
The ultimate price of freedom they did pay.

For Our Sister

Your body was still and quiet that day
As in mother's caring and loving arms you lay
While the truck sped along the narrow village streets
Horns blaring, urging all to clear the way.

But all our desperate attempts failed that day
As you inhaled your last precious breath
Your frail body giving up its defiant fight
Succumbing to the cruel hands of death.

Death's cold hands had finally grabbed you
And your body lay still and lifeless on the bed
Time seemed to stop as tears sadly flowed
For we then realized that indeed you were dead.

And as if by some divine intervention
Daddy's voice was heard down the corridor
But it was suddenly stilled and subdued
When he walked through that hospital door.

Death had conquered your small innocent body
We never thought you would leave us so soon
But your Heavenly Father above had called you
To your home in Heaven, that Sunday afternoon.

He had called you to your home dear Glorine
To dance, run and play with his angels above
Taking away all the pain and suffering of this earth
So you could enjoy his endless and wondrous love.

De Goliath

What happen? You 'fraid to say de word!
Man say it loud. Hurricane David!
It cannot come back an' hit you.
So you 'fraid say a hurricane name?
Even if your house go now!
Is true, David was bad. But even me was 'fraid.
When David start to blow like a dragon
An' trees ben' an' sway an' fall like matchstick
Who say I wasn' 'fraid?

When house fall like is with san' dey make
An' roof was breakin' an' flyin' to de sea
Like dey was aeroplane,
An' river flowin' like mad
An' de sea bouncin' on de shore
Threatenin' to take all house.
Who say I wasn' 'fraid?

But when I see people runnin' from dey house
An' David not stoppin', I was more 'fraid.
Yes man.
Doh laugh.
But I doh 'fraid now.
You talkin' like your mouth paralyze.
You is de ekonomy non?
I know de ekonomy paralyze but not your mouth!
An' where you goin' now? You still 'fraid?
Oh, you goin' for your rations!

Giftus R. John

Look man, look; doh tremble so
Like you still sufferin' from shock.
Come on, shake up. David will not come back.
You doh hear it breakup. It finish.

I know is true. It really was a demon.
But you know what?
David come to do a job jus' like in de good book.
He come to destroy goliath.
De goliath of hatred, fraud, political strife
Corruption an' malpractice
De goliath dat people supportin'
Because it look strong an' mighty.
Now we see how de goliath fall
An' so easy!

Let Freedom Ring

Let Freedom ring.
Let Freedom ring from the green tops
Of Diablotin.
Let Freedom ring
And let the bells of Freedom
Ring in this Land.
Let them toll all day long.

Let Peace flow.
Let Peace flow from
The Fresh Water and Boerie Lakes.
Let Peace flow
And let the clear waters of Peace
Flow in this Land.
Let Peace flow in torrents.

Let Justice fly.
Let Justice fly on the wings
Of the Sisserou Parrot.
Let justice fly all over this Land
And let Justice fly undisturbed.
Let corruption, injustice, oppression
Be thrown into the gaping mouth
Of the Boiling Lake
Never to be seen again.
Let them burn and be buried forever.

Giftus R. John

But let Love, Unity and Understanding
Blow from the heart of the forest
Of this Land.
Let them blow in the breeze
And let them blow over all men,
Especially the unjust.

Let Freedom ring,
Let Peace flow.
Let Justice fly.
And
Let Love, Unity and Understanding
Prevail in this Land.
From the tops of Diablotin
From the Lakes of Water
On the wings of the Sisserou
And let them pay heed.
But burn and bury
Oppression,
Injustice,
Greed,
Corruption.
And
Let Freedom Ring!

Snowfall

Just another morning
As the snowflakes fall
Softly landing on the bare tree limbs
And on the grass in the yard below.

The little boy presses his face
Against the cold window pane
Wishing he could catch the flakes
As they quickly drift past his window.

His bright eyes follow each snowflake
As it floats effortlessly down
Only to disappear among thousands more
Now lying on the grassy floor.

It's the first snowfall he's ever seen
For it never snows on his native isle
And this white stuff now falling to the ground
Amazes him more and more.

The snowfall becomes heavier and steadier
And the yard, once covered in green
Is now nothing more
But a sheet of white.

The brightness of the day
Slowly begins to fade away
As the storm clouds
Snuff out the early morning light.

Giftus R. John

His vantage point now begins getting cloudy
As his warm breath now condenses
On the cold window panes, slowly
Obscuring his curious view.

But he's grown tired now
The excitement has faded away
And slowly he steps down from his bed
To find something else to do.

The Island Man Sings His Song

The island man sings his song
In a land he now calls his own.
He sings his song of pain and suffering
In a land far, far away from home.

The island man sings his song
As he battles every day to survive.
In a land that's unforgiving
He keeps struggling to stay alive.

The island man sings his song
Daring never at all to stop;
Doing the best he possibly can
To own a house, raise a family, hold a job.

From dawn to dusk, noon to midnight
In rain or snow, sun or sleet
He sings his song of hope even if
He's forever on his aching feet.

The island man sings his song
For sadly he can do no less
To overcome the trials and obstacles
Forever standing in his path to success.

But yet the island man sings his song
A song of hope, a song of glory
For with all that lies before him
He keeps giving to his God the glory.

Giftus R. John

But he's determined to make it happen
As he works day and night, trying to cope,
Trying his utmost to make ends meet
As he sings his song. His song of Hope.

The Ghetto Song

In the ghetto
Tribulations, poverty, hunger, starvation
In the ghetto
Where masses
Trod on, push on, fight on
Against all forces…
The forces of oppression
And rejection.
In the ghetto
People search for an identity
No matter what the cost.
In the ghetto
Barefooted children playing,
Bellies bulging
From malnutrition.
Smoke fills the air
While music soothes the ear.
Reggae music of the rastaman
Giving inspiration to the ghetto child
A hungry child
Tugging at a mother's dress.
A child growing wild
In the ghetto.
Rastaman locks swing in the air
And the smell of the chalice
Fills the ghetto
A ghetto filled with fear
Anguish and pain.
The ghetto cry
Resounds over and over again.

Giftus R. John

The cry of the ghetto brothers and sisters.
The cry of the ghetto people.
People searching for an answer
To their identity
A true black identity
In the ghetto.
An identity lost
Mangled, destroyed, sabotaged.
Yet they keep searching
Determined to find
That identity.
And they keep hearing the echo.
The echo in the ghetto
Over and over
And over again.

Faces

Faces
All kinds
Smiling
Sleepy
Surprised
Lost.
White
Black
Asian
Hispanic.
Faces.
Men
Women
Children.
Cold.
Facing each other
Cuddled
Against each other
Feeling
Each other's warmth.
Faces.
A squeal
A rattle
A rumble
A flash of light
In the dark tunnel.
The sound of iron wheels
Racing along the tracks.

Giftus R. John

Hard bucket seats below your tired butt.
A stinking bum huddled in a corner,
A newspaper hiding his face
And his intentions.
An open bottle in a brown bag
Rolling from side to side
With the motions of the train
Its contents, leaking out
Making a mess,
On the already dirty floor.
Rap music blares
From a boombox
Somewhere in the back of the car
The warning signs blatantly ignored.
Who cares anymore!
A woman polishes her face
Using her pocket mirror.
Like a sculptor
She puts on the finishing touches
Before her stop.
Dull faces.
Faces stuck in novels
Textbooks
Newspapers
Anything.
Some
Seeing nothing,
Reading nothing.
Just staring…
Faces.
Faces of the city
Faces of the morning.
The train comes to a screeching stop.

The Island Man Sings His Song

The conductor opens the doors
And they rush out
Like a loose herd
Each into a world of their own.
In this subterranean jungle.
Faces.
The conductor looks up,
Looks down and up again.
All is clear on the platform.
"Watch the closing doors.
Next stop 42nd Street".
She slams her window shut.
As the train slowly eases off the station
And rumbles on again
Into the dark bowels of the city.

Visions

Somewhere
In the innermost crevices of my mind
Something is formed
Somewhere deep within
Another life lives.
Deep down.

Somewhere
In the innermost senses
I see a new me
A different me
A me crying out
For something
Craving to reach out and hold
Touch, change
What I know, what I see.
But the undulating wave lengths
Fail to reach out to you
And I stand alone, wondering
Whether the visions I see
Deep within
Can be true.

For deep inside
Past all the crevices and shadows
In the depths of my mind
Another me takes shape
Another me is formed.
It shimmers
Then slowly fades away.
A vision of you.

They Riot in the City Tonight

There was a riot in the city tonight
A riot between blacks and whites.
There was a riot in the city tonight
A cry for justice from Brooklyn Heights.

There was a riot in the city tonight
Blacks fighting for their civil rights.
There was a riot in the city tonight
And that for sure was no pretty sight.

Justice! Equal Rights! Was their call
As they marched against police might.
Peace! Justice! Equality! For all
They kept chanting through the night.

Mindless of the flying sticks and stones
They're fighting for their rights tonight.
Heedless of broken limbs and bones
They're fighting in the city tonight.

Tonight they hold the place at siege
As they march in the city tonight.
From Bensonhurst to The Brooklyn Bridge
They're fighting for their human rights.

Oh what a sight in the city tonight
The pressure's getting rather tight
The blacks cry out for equal rights
So they riot in New York City tonight.

Summertime Nostalgia

The smell of the freshly mowed
Dew covered grass
Fills the cool morning air
As the low mist
Engulfs the tall coconut tress
Standing like sentinels keeping watch over the area.

The roosters greet the morning
From their lofty perches
Their raspy crowing sounding from everywhere.
Birds chirp noisily from
Cedar and fruit tress, jumping from
Blossom to blossom sucking at the sweet-tasting nectar.

The sun's rays lazily crawl
Across the still damp yard
Dotted here and there with chicken droppings.
At the office daddy takes the roll call
Before assigning the day's duties
To the men and women who are under his care.

It's another start to another summer's day
As mother feeds the fireplace
With pieces of *galba* and *gommier*.
The smoke fills the small kitchen
Before escaping through the ceiling vents;
Swirling and disappearing into the cool morning air.

The Island Man Sings His Song

Box trucks, loaded with passengers
And goods for market, snake their way
Slowly along the winding banks of the Layou River.
Drivers blast their horns as they approach
The narrow winding corners.
It's another summer's morning at Cocoa Center.

A farmer, headed to his plantation in the hills,
Stops by to collect cocoa and citrus seedlings
That he'll plant and nurture.
And hopefully in time, these plants,
They'll grow tall and strong in the fertile soil
Bearing fruit aplenty for that farmer.

The cattle bellow as they are taken
To pasture by "Ole Man Hambo"
While the calves skip and jump wildly about
Alarming the chickens feasting on a meal of
Grated coconuts and growing marsh
Causing them to scatter in fear.

Behind the tall hedge at the overseer's home
I hear the voices of his kids;
They're here for the summer
Like they always do, leaving
Roseau with its lights and glitter
For a few weeks, to be here.

Today we will roam all over the estate
And mingle with the workers as they plant and dig.
We'll run along the raised cobble stone paths
Pushing each other in a rickety wheelbarrow
Up the hill and down again as we sweat
Profusely, in the sweltering heat.

Giftus R. John

Today we will chase a wild hen away
Capturing her young brood
Taking them to the sanctuary of daddy's brooder
Lest they become easy victims
Of a hungry, *tete chien,* coiled and ready,
Or to some low flying hawk, a sumptuous treat.

Today we will walk to the river
Where we will collect mangoes
That have fallen from the trees lining its banks
Lodged among the stones
In the shallow clear rushing water.
We'll bathe till we hear the shouts
Of mother or the overseer's cook
Beckoning us to come home to eat.

Today we'll fill our bellies with
Guavas, cherries, grapefruits and even dry coconuts
And when no one is looking
A red juicy tomato straight from the vine
In those huge propagation bins
Letting the warm tacky juices
Run down our chins and fingers
As we bite into the meat.

It's just another summer's day at Cocoa center
Until the sun disappears over the Senjo hills
And night takes hold.
As darkness slowly descends on the estate.
The birds and fowls, noisily chirping and crackling,
Seek sanctuary among the branches of
The tall trees spread all over.

The Island Man Sings His Song

The crickets begin hissing as the
Fireflies dot the landscape
With their blinking phosphorous lights and
The frogs croak somewhere in the distance.
But the stillness of the night slowly begins to triumph
Marking the end of yet
Another summer's day at Cocoa Center.

Who am I?

Who am I?
Really, who am I?
I am the child
Who never knew
What it was to be alive;
Murdered before I was born
As I lay helpless in my mother's womb.

Who am I?
I am the child,
The hungry child in the corner
Craving for a meal,
Craving for new shoes
To cover my feet
From the rain and winter's bitter cold.

Who am I?
I am the vet
Who fought to defend
My country and its allies;
Their rights and their freedoms.
Yet my reward
A lonely, unmarked and forgotten tomb.

The Island Man Sings His Song

Who am I?
I am the refugee
Fleeing from my own country
Overtaken by tyrants,
Riddled by war and starvation,
Robbed of its people.
Robbed of its diamonds and its gold.

Who am I?
I am the homeless one
Sleeping on the city streets
While around me
Standing like ghosts,
Abandoned and deserted buildings;
Sad reflections of our daily plight and doom.

Who am I?
I am me, I am you
Searching for an answer
As the days grow old
Searching for an answer
To unanswered questions.
Searching for answers to stories yet untold.

The Royal Palm

By the busy village roadside
This royal palm stood alone
Tall, leafless and branchless
Seen but yet still quite unknown.

In years alas gone by
I was the pillar of admiration
Swaying as it was photographed
By visitors from many a nation.

But all beauty faded away
And it became dull and old
Standing out there alone
First scorched, then wet and cold.

No one regarded it then
No one even ever noticed
Only a poet remembered
As the royal palm slowly died.

Its fruits we no longer gather
Nor do the high-flying birds nestle.
Its life goes on no further
It has ceased without a rustle.

For a few years more
The strong skeleton stood
Till destruction came its way
Sadly cut for use as firewood.

The Island Man Sings His Song

Today, all that's left
Is a rotting hollow stump
The only remembrance
Of a giant Royal Palm.

Face of Darkness

A glowing sky,
A sinking ball,
A slow flying seagull,
A canoe proceeding slowly toward shore,
The silent splash of the waves
Against the black rocks.
The shrill notes
Of a nestling bird,
The distant sound of a moving vehicle,
The hissing sound of
The night insects
And the rustling leaves.
All,
Seen or heard.
They crown a fine day,
A sad day;
Yet be it what it was
The end is near
For the face of darkness is being revealed
Being heralded.
Slowly they all disappear.
Sky, bird, sun, canoe are seen no more
Only the sound of the splashing water
Against the rocks
And of the rustling leaves
Are heard
As
The Face of Darkness
Slowly unveils itself.

The City

The riots are long gone
Yet the wounds linger on
In a city growing beyond its borders
In a world of uncertainty
As another day draws to an end.
The looting and shootings have long gone
Yet the pain still lingers on
Within a city where houses of worship are nestled
Among bars, watering holes and nightclubs.
A city where billboards spell out
The values of their respective products
From the walls and roofs of buildings
As the pastors urge their flock to turn away from the
Pleasures of this world and save their souls,
While the congregations raise their voices in unison
Singing and swaying to their favorite Negro spirituals.
Addicts and homeless sit
Around a makeshift table
Numbing their frustration
With a sip of booze in a vacant lot
Filled with the rusting carcasses of old cars
Now overgrown with weeds and shrubs.
Dilapidated high rise buildings,
Once the hope of low-cost housing,
Implode like the frustration and despair
Of their now homeless inhabitants,
Crashing to the ground in clouds of dust.

Giftus R. John

Teenagers run carefree through life's journey
Procreating and rearing innocent ones
To a doomed life in a city
Where the shells of the vacant buildings
Pervade the darkened skyline.
Where garbage strewn backyards, alleys and streets
Become playgrounds for rats and mice and children too,
Amid empty beer cans and broken bottles,
Used tires, condoms and coke vials.
The police siren still wail
As they chase juvenile car thieves
Raising hell on the dark end of the streets,
Smoking pot, making "donuts" and popping their illegal guns
Holding the citizens hostage through the night.
Life in the city gets bogged down with its
Overcrowded schools and lack of health care
Run down and crime-ridden housing projects,
The stumping grounds and battlefields of drug rivals
Laying claim to their *turf*.
Like sphinxes from the ashes,
New houses rise,
Dotting the city's landscape
Signaling hope for the future of its people
Where life seems nothing but a thing granted
Yet to be wasted away by some individuals
Whose dreams lay shattered on the sidewalk
Like the remnants from a broken window
Of yet another stolen car.
In the distant, a jetliner drones as it climbs
Through the darkness,
Its takeoff lights shining brightly
Through the clouds,
Showing the way.

The Island Man Sings His Song

The deafening roar
Of its powerful engines
Resound through the night
As it soars overhead
And a city prepares
For what now lies ahead
For yet another night.

The Sun Sets on A Nation's Son

A voice has been stilled
A hero struck down
And a nation mourns
As it bids a sad farewell to a famous son.

Dusk settles over the Land
As the winds of change have stalled
And a nation fervently prays as its leader,
From this world has now been called.

A student? A radical? A troublemaker?
A leftist? A communist? A leader?
Who was he?
To Portsmouth a son…to George William an instigator
To Libya, Grenada and Cuba a revolutionary brother.
To all of us Rosie!!

A man of the people,
A man with a vision,
A passion for change,
Working against the political grain;
Moving beyond the dreams
Of a young country and its naïve leaders
Not yet ready to accept the radical ideologies
Of one singing the leftist refrain.

A voice has been stilled
And a people sadly mourn.
Friends, foes, comrades
Grieve the fall of a warrior, one so bold.

The Island Man Sings His Song

The people's leader, the people's voice
Struck down before he could
His dreams, his hopes and aspirations,
For this young island nation, mold.

No more with us
No more to express his thoughts
No more to expound his fiery dialogues
And ideologies, on this country's political stage.

Now he lives us to dream
Not of what if and what could be
But to dream of what can be and
Turn still yet in our checkered history, another page.

The sun has set for him now
And sadly we say goodbye
And hope that we'll move on once more
As our nation weeps and ponders its future.

Now the people bid farewell to a Son
As Dominica and the Caribbean mourn
The loss, so soon, so sudden, so swift
Of a friend, a comrade, a leader, a brother.

Me Gold

Me trod in de bad muddy road
On me scalp a heavy load
What? A bunch of green gold
Me bananas goin' to be sold.

Me trek in mud an' rain
No shoe on me large stumpy feet
Cuttin' me precious green fingas
Laborin' under de scorchin' heat.

Me back breakin', me head achin'
Oh Lord please help me.
I can't go on, I can't stop
Me dyin', me tired, me thirtsty.

Carry de bananas to me truck
Till me get a full load
An' den me leave for de boxin' plant
Drivin' real careful on de windin' road.

When me arrive me unpack
Put all me load on de ground
Takin' all me care brudda
For dese fingas dey de best I ever found.

Me spend so long in de boxin' plant
Me hungry, me tired waitin'.
Dem selectors dey aint busy
All a dem me time waistin'.

The Island Man Sings His Song

Dey pick up me nice hands
Look at dem from tip to crown
Turn dem face in all kind o' way
An den dey pass dem on.

At las me finish an' me headin' home
But what nex'? Me money!
A little change is all me gonna get
Why Lord, please tell me?

Dem englanders dey aint know fig
Dem refuse all we good fruit
Sayin' dem bruise, dem ugly.
Dem englanders wid all de loot.

But all a dat aint really so
'Cause one day me gonna hear dem cry
An' den me gonna refuse to sell
But tell me? Can I?

Marooned

Hoarded, chained, beaten,
Lashed, pushed, cargoed
To the barracoons
Separated from my brothers
From my family.

Loaded on a ship,
Sailing
Along a passage
Of torture,
Of agony,
Of starvation,
Of death.
Along a passage of
Blue emptiness.

My brothers cry
My brothers are beaten
My brothers starve
My brothers die around me.

Strange lands appear
They are different, unknown to me.
They come closer
And there I am sold
Sold to white
Sold to brutality
Sold for a few dollars
Sold to my death in alien grounds
Sold to SLAVERY.

The Island Man Sings His Song

I toiled and toiled.
Worse than a horse.
Lashed like an ass.
No pity for me, no mercy.
Made to suffer
In snake-covered sugar cane fields.
Lashed
By my brothers.
My own brothers.

Still I suffer
I am tortured, I am brutalized
Forced to change
My way of life
Forced to follow
Corrupt styles
Forced to follow one that is alien to me.

Still I am a slave
Marooned from my Motherland
Marooned from
Mother Africa.

Midnight Melody

Dogs barking
                Donkeys braying
                                Roosters crowing
                                              In the mid of night.

Am I Me?

Am I me?
Am I myself?
Am I the one I think I am?
　　The one I ought to be?
　　The one I hope to be?

Am I the one
With the God-given rights
Freedom, understanding
Peace of mind?

Am I the one
Who has to stand up
Against injustice, oppression, corruption.
Against racism?

Am I the one
Free to smell
The early morning grass
Free to touch
The beautiful flowers of nature
Free to drink
The pure clear water?

Am I the one
With the right to live
As I ought to
Speak as I hope to?

Giftus R. John

Am I that one?
Am I myself?
Am I me?

A Symbol

Look at him
Clad in his heavy suit,
His neat blocks.
See him
Symbol of the easy living ones.

See him
Cruising in his new limousine.
What does he stand for?
Injustice, Oppression, Lust for Power.

See him
Symbol of the Power Thirsty maniac.
See him
A symbol of favor winners.
And see him
His hands rough, torn, cut.
His feet bare, hard, strong.
See him a symbol of a hard worker
Symbol of a toiler
Symbol of the roots man
Symbol of the island's foundation
Symbol of the island's masses.

And see him
Him without a meal
Him without a home
Him without a pair of pants
Without a shirt
Except for the ones he wears all year round.

Giftus R. John

See him
Hungry, starving, dying.
See him
Symbol of the sufferer
Symbol of the oppressed
Symbol of the unwanted
Symbol of the dying.

See them all
Members of our society.
A society disjointed by class, power
Status, beliefs, color
A society disjointed through selfishness
Greed and politics
A society heading
Towards a new path.
A new light
A new avenue
A new birth.

The Fight Must Go on

I have lived in torment.
I have suffered in my fight
My fight for equality, for humanity.
Politically assassinated,
Branded as a traitor, as a radical
As a communist.
I have been pulled in behind bars
Locked up in filthy stinking cells;
Manhandled, maltreated.
Rejected because I fight
For my brothers
Who suffer unceasingly.

Can't stop my fight
Even though I have been brutalized
By a set of criminals in disguise.
No, I won't stop.

Tear-gassed, shot at
I won't budge.
Why should I let things
Which affect me,
Which affect the black man
Continue to go on?

Giftus R. John

They'll shoot me, imprison me, starve me
But I won't stop.
Like a scar left after a burn
I'll always be there.
My brothers must carry on
They too fight for their rights.

I'll be dead and gone
Buried, rotten six feet below
But alive, alive will I be
In the hearts and minds
Of my fellowmen.
We shall fight to the very end.
The fight must go on.

New Light

The waters of the blue Caribbean
Rush towards the rocky shores
And disintegrates into a sheet of white
As it rushes back, after impact.

A bright tropic sun
Lazily crawls
Over the misty hills,
Brightening the sky
    And all in its path.

A people
    Rush about in their own contortions
And a new nation rises
And its people are reborn
As its children sing,
As its culture is expressed,
As its people struggle
For their Freedom,
    As its people die
For their freedom,
    As its people herald
The coming light.

Search

Search my mind, yes go on, search
In its vastness, in its numerous chambers
You'll find questions, answers.
Open it, search.

Search my mind, yes search
And in its chambers
You'll find hidden, deep down
A number of puzzles, problems.
Open it, search.

Search my mind, yes, search
And in its deep dark caves
You'll find well sealed thoughts
Too precious to let out.
Open it, search.

Search and when you're over
Be careful that you do not distort
Its machinery
Lest you be lost in its deep chambers,
Search.

For if you search my mind
You'll wonder why I act as I do,
Why I ask questions,
Why the black man has to suffer
Suffer under the hands of his fellowmen

The Island Man Sings His Song

But then you'll see
That in my mind, there flows
A stream of unending thoughts;
Thoughts that help to create
My mind's stability.
So search, search and keep searching.

We're Coming Back

I felt a touch, a slight cold touch
And I heard a voice, a rough eerie voice.
I trembled, I shook
But still my eyes were shut;
And the voice spoke to me.

"Go out and tell the black man
Tell them we are coming back
Coming back for revenge,
Revenge for what happened
On the sugar plantations."

My blood drew cold, my mind went blank
And the voice it continued.

"Tell them Cuffy will return
And when he returns
We will burn and fight
We'll fight for our rights
We'll die for our rights."

I opened my mouth to shout
To shout for help
But it stayed shut
And the voice it became louder.

"And tell them that Jacko is coming back."

The Island Man Sings His Song

The walls seemed to cave in,
Cave in on me
And the roof seemed to be falling,
Falling slowly
And I felt the touch once more
As the voice sank to a murmur.

"Tell them Luther, Marcus, Bogle and Malcolm
Are coming back
Coming to put the lands straight.
Go now, we cannot wait."

I raised my hand
And it fell back limply.
I opened my eyes
And as the voice slowly drifted away
I still heard it saying,

"Go out
Tell the rulers,
Tell the black man,
Tell the whites,
Tell them all.
Tell them we have waited till now
And we are returning
And the black man will sing his song
His song of Freedom
For we are coming back.

Yes Martin, Bogle, Cuffy, Malcolm and I."

Giftus R. John

A cock crowed,
A frightening sound…
I felt weak.
I looked around
And as the first rays of the sun
Sipped into my bedroom
I still could hear the faint voice.

"We are coming to set things straight
We cannot wait.
We are coming back
And we'll sing our song
Our Song of Freedom."

Old African Man

The smoke from his pipe
Climbs like in sacrifice to his god
As it mingles with
The rays of the evening sun.

Old man, descendant of an African village
Old man descendant of a captured African
In whose blood flows
The rhythm of the drums
The rhythm of the African dance and chant.

He sits on a stone
Under the breadfruit tree
Where he's told many an African story,
Sang many an African song
Under the moonlight,
While the children intently listened.

Old man whose body has been wracked
By the labors in the hot West Indian sun,
Old man whose hands have rocked the village
As he beat on the drums
And the women danced and chanted.
Old man of an African village.
He has dug the earth
Planted the crops
And his powerful legs plodded
As he bore the fruits of his labors
To his family.

Giftus R. John

Now he sits quietly
And gazes at the sun
Sinking below the horizon.
He puffs at his pipe
As if in praise to his god
Waiting for the inevitable end.

Old man, old African man.

You, The Poem

I write this poem
Not to be read,
Nor to be talked about
But to be loved.

For I write this poem
Because you are
The Poem,
The Poem that I love.

You on whose face
I see everything.
You on whose face
I write the sweetest words
You on whose face
Lie the questions that
I ask
The answers that
I get.
You, the Poem that I love.

You in whom everything I feel
Stays, lives and grows
Just because I love you,
You, the Poem.
You, whose presence creates
A new day, a new life.
You are the letters, the words
The lines of my life.
You, the Poem that I love.

A Confused World

This world really seems to be no more
What we everyday pray and long for
There is so much happening in every nation.
What a sad and dreadful situation.

There is no honesty in men's hearts
As we tear each other apart
While every day man tries doing away
With any one standing in his way.

World leaders talk of conquests
And so they try out nuclear tests,
Pollution of air and drinking water
Is what results when it's all over.

Young men are killed in useless wars
While governments impose harmful laws
Curtailing people's rights and freedoms
As their own nations they hold ransom.

There's no ease in racial tensions
Among all kins, tribes and nations
Blacks, Whites, Jews, Muslims, Christians
No one wants to extend a loving hand.

Innocent people are kidnapped
Planes blown apart or hijacked
And the offenders asking for ransoms
As in foreign lands they seek asylum.

The Island Man Sings His Song

Those who speak for their human rights
Are arrested, beaten, put out of sight
Cast away, left to rot in a dark prison cell
Their lives now nothing but a living hell.

The young and old are at odds with each other
Sometimes it makes me stop and ponder.
The young say right, the old say wrong
And so the struggle goes on and on.

But we hope someday there will be peace
From Cambodia to Kosovo, to the Middle East
And we hope that somehow, someday
Someone listens to what the people say.

Lord Me Wan' Pray

Lord, me wan' pray today
Dat you show me de way
As me go about me way.
And so me wan' pray
For me kids dem too.
Yes me got two
Like you know an'
Me wan' dem to grow up de right way
Yes Lord.
'Cause in de world today
Got so much ting to
Lead dem astray.
Yes Lord
Is sometin' different everyday.
Dem chilren of today
Dem out ah control
Plenty of dem done loss dey soul awready.
And den dem say dem chilren not 'spose
To pray in school.
But lord
Dem killin' each other
Dem hurtin' each other
Dem abusin' each other
Dem shootin' each other
In de same school where dem not prayin'.
But den de politicians dem
Say dat de state an' de church
Not 'spose be together in de same place an' de same time.
So who go teach dem de golden rule?

The Island Man Sings His Song

Me tink dis is a disgrace.
Oh yes Lord me really tink so.
So Lord me ask you
To guide me kids dem along de way.
An' me wan' pray
For me mudda an' me fadda dem
Back in de island
In de West Indies.
An' me pray for me brudda an' sista dem also
Help dem Lord, an' dem kids too.
An' me wan' a pray
For all ah we, oh yes Lord
All ah de people everywhere
'Cause Lord, terrible tings happenin' dose days.
We got
War in de Middle Eas' an'
War in Afrika,
War in Kosovo an'
War in Bosnia.
Infac' Lord, is war everywhere
Even in our hearts.
An' if it no have war
Den is earthquake, or flood
Or hurricane or big fire 'pon de land.
Or is a plane hijack or drop from de sky
Or a suicide bomber blow up a buildin'
Killin' innocent people.
Or somebody sen' a missile over
Somebody else country.
Or some big oil tanker run agroun' in de ocean
An' all de oil leak out
Causin' pollution an' destroyin'
De wildlife.

Giftus R. John

Lord,
Is sometin' different everyday.
So me pray
Today an' everyday.
Yes Lord, me go down on me knees
An' me pray
Cause dem still have discrimination,
Racism an' segregation
After all dem years
An' after all dem man who
Fight to end it
Pay for it with dem life.
Yes Lord
Dey still call us nigga.
Dey still no wan' give us we chance
To show we on de same level wid dem.
Dey like to see us
Dribble de basketball,
Hit de homerun,
Run like de wind,
Score a touchdown,
Knock out de opponent,
So dey can scream at de top of dey voice
Cause dey care bout dey team, not us.
But Lord dey no want us
To live near dem home
Or work in dey office
When de day is over.
When we move in,
Dey move out.
When we move in,
Dey sen dey kids to another school.
Or dey move to another town.

The Island Man Sings His Song

But Lord me no gonna change
De color of me skin.
Me not gonna change
Me hair either
It rough an' kinky…
Been like dat since de day me was born.
Me black, me from Africa
Or Dominica,
Or wherever dey wan' to say me come from.
But me like me color.
Look at me Lord, me color nice!
Me no have to worry bout gettin' tan
Me no have to sit all day in de sun
Cause me tan awready.
Me tan from de day you make me.
So Lord me pray
For me an' me people again
Me pray 'cause Lord e'en me black
Some still tink me not one of dem
'Cause me from de islands.
See, dem say since me not from Amerika
Me is alien.
Like me is some unknown
From outa space
Like ET.
Funny dey say dat
'Cause we no call none a dem alien.
When dey come to we country
We no call dem alien
We call dem turists…
But Lord dis is we cross and we
Have to carry it 'pon we shoulder
Just like you carry you cross for we.

Giftus R. John

So Lord today me pray
Me pray dat you hear me Lord
Me no wan' shout
Me jus' wan' a whisper
So me no lose control of meself.
Me does get me emotions up sometimes
An' it no good for me
Oh yes Lord me does get riled up
When me tink bout all a dis
'Cause Lord it no look like it
Goin stop anytime.
We jus destroyin' we self.
Lord it so sad!.
So me pray Lord
Help me today
Along me way.
Amen an' Amen.

My Day

The sun's up
I wake up
I bathe up
I dress up
I eat up
I run out
I drive out
I drive up
I speed up
I pay up
I park up
I pay up
I run up…the platform
I get on
I stand up
I get out
I run up
I sign in
I sit down
I work…non-stop.
I sign out
I run out
It's dark out….

Play Ball!

The tarp has been taken off
And batting practice is over
The fielders are in position
Everyone's now ready to play.

The ump signals time to play ball
And the crowd cheers wildly
As the batter in the box
Gets set to hit away.

It's a strike. It's a ball.
An error, a pass ball.
A base hit, a homer.
Strike him out. Throw him out…

First timers and regulars
Old timers and day patrons
From the mezzanine to the bleachers
They all wave, scream and shout.

Popcorn and crackerjack
Soda, beer and cotton candy
Ice cream, peanuts and a few hotdogs too.
There's a lot of everything.

Seventh inning stretch time
And thousands of voices roar lustily
The music reverberates throughout the stadium
While on the diamond the ground crew does its thing.

The Island Man Sings His Song

A brush back pitch too near the chin
And the batter glares back in disbelief
A foul ball flies into the stands
A souvenir it is for some lucky fan.

Summer, and it's baseball once again
Under a blazing August sun.
At the old ball park in the Bronx,
It's time for all to have some fun.

The Snow Storm

The boiler's running, the heat is on
Outside it's snowing, the storm is on
The schools are closed, we have no class
We're both home today and we're loving it.

Daddy's outside, he's shoveling snow
Mammy's in the kitchen, making us tea
They're home also, for they can't go to work
It's too risky driving out of town.

Soon we'll go outside and run about
Build a snowman, ride a sled
Make some snowballs, slip and slide
Play with our friends across the street.

The snow is falling, upon our heads
The plows are coming, down our street
They're piling the snow, along the curb
Spreading sand and salt as they roll along.

The wind is blowing; it's rather strong
Our toes are numb, our cheeks are cold
So inside we go, we need some warmth
Mammy's got something hot for us to eat.

Down in the basement, we gather then
It's nice and warm; how we love it there!
We'll read a book, play some games
Listen to some music and sing along.

The Island Man Sings His Song

The sun is out, the wind has stopped
Our neighbors are out, cleaning their cars
The tough task ahead they're ready to face
With shovels in hand and boots on their feet.

The night draws closer as darkness falls
The streetlights come on one by one
Dimly flickering on and off and on again
Thank God, for now the storm is gone.

Remembering Aurora

Many passed through your doors
As the years went by
And many sat on the wooden benches
Diligently repeating their tables and lines.

Time was when you were
The pride and joy of the village
Standing proudly alone out there, on the hill
As by all you were admired.

Many a fond memory still treasure
Of their years under your roof
As they worked to gain an education
Within your hot, crowded and modest confines.

But no one cared, no one worried
You were the best among the rest
And without fail, day after day
For the very best we all aspired.

We remember many a headmaster
Who tirelessly toiled under your roof
Great memories of strong and devoted men
Who taught till the sun went down.

John-Rose chasing late comers through the yard
Georges, playing rousing tunes
On his cherished violin, as we sang along
And Thomas who was a great man to meet.

The Island Man Sings His Song

Yet there were others too, not to be forgotten
Who left their indelible marks upon your walls
They're all gone now and so too the symbol
The beautiful symbol of the Rising Sun.

You meant so much to all of us
A place to meet, a place to learn,
Where the young gathered in the shade
Seeking refuge from the afternoon heat.

We remember the sound of the bell
Beckoning all to come right in
Or its welcome sound at the end of the day
When out the doors to our homes we'd go.

The voices in the building are forever stilled
And we no longer join to pray and sing
Share each other's aches, our pains and joys.
As we were openly spanked, chastised or praised.

A place where we sat, a place
Where we had fun, where we laughed,
Where on many a Sunday afternoon we congregated,
Enjoying a cricket game played on the field below.

But the memories will live on forever
As we remember you, Aurora
Even though into the sunset you have faded
With hardly a fanfare or flag being raised

The River's Gone

Giant tree trunks lie
Buried deep within
The mounds of sand piled high,
Where water once flowed on down.
Tall trees lining the banks,
Seem praying for the river
To release her prized possession.
But the river's gone.

Where once fish of every kind swam
Zipping, and jumping, splashing about
In deep pools of aqua blue.
So deep many a soul dared not
Its prowess test, as it flowed on.
Waters seemingly so calm and placid
Before cascading noisily
Over jagged rocks and stones.
But it's dry now and nothing flows.
The river's gone.

Where many dove and swam
Through the years
Where we watched in awe
As the swollen waters rushed madly on.
Tree trunks tossed wildly about
Having been ripped from the ground
Along its soggy banks.
But now the river's gone.

The Island Man Sings His Song

The fury has been calmed
No more the music
Of the rushing crystal clear water
On a bright early morn
Nor the rustling tunes of bamboo leaves
Growing along the water's edge…
On a bright moonlit night.
Where has the River gone?

Yea it's gone
The once powerful and feared
Meandering along its numerous bends and curves
Way up from the dense canopies
As it journeyed out to meet the sea.
It's gone now, sad to say,
A victim of man and nature…
Unable to defend herself, even as she cried out.
But she's gone.
The River's gone to eternity.

Sunday Afternoon

The sun's rays beam down to earth
And there is not a breeze blowing
From the sea, or even from the valleys
To help soothe this hot and restless being.

A speeding truck roars quickly by
Causing everyone in the street to flee.
Frightening even some of the old folks
Relaxing in the shade of a breadfruit tree.

A domino player slams down his hand
And the wooden table squeaks at its joints.
"Doh isi! Doh isi!" he shouts jubilantly
As his partner collects the losers' points.

"Mouche ka allé en manjé la, ti monde"
A young mother screams at her little boy
But he pays no heed to her urgent pleas
And keeps playing with his brother's toy.

"Ice Cream! Peanuts! Taste me now!"
A street vendor now shouts aloud
Her tray of goodies perched on her head
As she moves among the Sunday crowd.

"Black pudding! Get your black pudding!"
Yet another vendor does loudly yell.
It seems like everyone in the village
Today has something they'd like to sell.

The Island Man Sings His Song

All this happens on a Sunday afternoon
As village life moves slowly by
All that on a hot Sunday afternoon
As the brilliant sun moves across the sky.

All that on another Sunday afternoon
As a lone fisherman now comes ashore
And though a futile trip to sea today
Tomorrow his luck he'll try once more.

All that, on yet another Sunday afternoon
While the kids a game of cards they play
Beneath the loft of the village church
And life in Senjo moves on yet another day.

Their Game

Chacala bang! Chacala bang!
The tin rings out
As the dice rolls
Sounding the call for the night.
Chacala bang!
Under the lamp post
On the street corner
As young men gather.

"Vini, vini"
A young man cries
As the December breeze
Blows cold from the valley
Softly rustling the leaves
Of the mango tree
On the riverbank.
"Vini" he cries louder.

"Double six!" "Hold it!" "Stop!"
They cry
As five cents, quarters,
Are placed on the wooden board.
The tin rings again
Chacala bang!
As they watch intently
While the dice rolls faster.

The Island Man Sings His Song

"Mwen isi, Mwen isi"
A young boy cries
As he wriggles his way in
But his stay is but a while
By a solid slap
Across his head.
"Allé ah kai!"
Orders his mother.

Some lose.
Others win.
A few look on curiously
Or stand around aimlessly.
Some walk away
Seemingly unperturbed
By what goes on
On the street corner.

The dice rolls again
"I win! I win!"
"So my quarter dere lose!"
"Whey my fifty cents?"
"Garcon give me my money!"
They scream and shout.
It's pure confusion
And it's getting louder.

Chacala bang! Chacala bang!
The dice rolls again.
"Place your bet guys!"
"Let's go fellas!"
The young man cries once more
As they slowly congregate
Under the lamp post
On the street corner.

Until Tomorrow

The gentle night breeze
Sweeps over the small sandy village
While the strums of a guitar
Resound somewhere as
Young voices in discordant notes
Chant a local folk song.

Flickers from kerosene lamps
Sip lazily through
Curtained windows and doors
Softly kissing the glistening branches
Of the palm leaves
Growing tall and strong.

On the shore the sea
Sings herself a song
As she slams against the moss covered rocks.
A pantless little boy runs to the water's edge
As the white-laced waves
Rush in and disappear in the dark.

The village grows quiet as
The guitar's throbbing beat
And the voices finally cease.
The silence takes over
Until tomorrow
When they will all be back.

About the Author

Giftus John was born in the village of. St. Joseph on the island of Dominica. He attended the St. Joseph Government School, The Saint Mary's Academy and Sixth Form College. It was while a student at St. Mary's that Giftus began writing. He contributed poems to the school's newspaper, *The Marian Messenger*, and to the island's local weekly newspaper, *The Star*.

He was the winner of both the National Day Poetry and Short Story Competitions in 1975.

The Island Man Sings His Song is a collection of poems expressing the author's perspective on various aspects of life in general: culture, romance, social concerns and life in the Caribbean and in the United States.

Giftus resides in Union, New Jersey.